Th

SPUR BOOK

of

SMALL BOAT HANDLING

Also in the
SPURBOOK VENTURE GUIDE SERIES . . .

The
SPUR BOOK
of
SMALL BOAT HANDLING

by
Terry Brown & Rob Hunter

SPURBOOKS LIMITED

Published by:
SPURBOOKS LIMITED
6 Parade Court
Bourne End
Buckinghamshire

ISBN 0 904978 74 5

Printed by Maund & Irvine Ltd., Tring, Herts.

CONTENTS

PUBLISHER'S INTRODUCTION

ABOUT THIS SERIES

Venture Guides are written for outdoor people of all ages, and fall into two broad areas. The first area is concerned with skills and covers the basic techniques and knowledge that all outdoor people should possess. It includes books on Knots and Splicing, on Map and Compass work, Weather Lore, First Aid, Survival and Rescue, Camping and Outdoor Cooking. The second area covers what we describe as Venture Sports, that is, activities which require little mechanical equipment and are not team games. This includes such activities as Sailing and Canoeing, Downhill and Cross-Country Skiing, Rock Climbing, Hill Walking and Backpacking, Snorkelling and Dinghy Cruising; Caving and Walking.

ABOUT THIS BOOK

This book is designed to advise and instruct on the techniques necessary to handle and maintain a small boat. Other books in this series deal with sailing dinghies (*Sailing* by Brown & Hunter; *Dinghy Cruising* by Margaret Dye) and Canoeing (*Wild Water Canoeing* by Fred Barlow) and we are concerned here with rowing boats and skiffs, small yacht tenders and praams, fishing craft, sports-boats, and the smaller inflatable craft. These boats may be propelled by oars, single paddles, by sculling or by small outboard engines. The range is vast, so we will stick firmly to these boundaries and give advice on techniques which will be generally useful in the broad mass of small boats and to their handlers.

Please note that to stay in line with common usage, measurements are given in a mixture of imperial and metric.

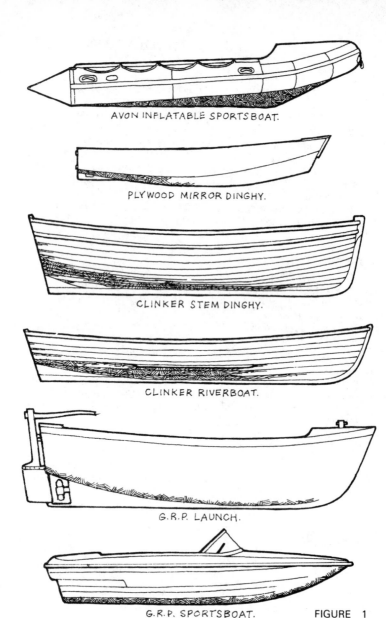

AVON INFLATABLE SPORTSBOAT.

PLYWOOD MIRROR DINGHY.

CLINKER STEM DINGHY.

CLINKER RIVERBOAT.

G.R.P. LAUNCH.

G.R.P. SPORTSBOAT.

FIGURE 1

Chapter 1

SMALL BOAT TYPES

We ought to define exactly what *we* mean by a small boat. Since the range of small craft is vast and there is no official definition, let us say that we define a small craft as 'small' by the following yardsticks:

1. A small boat is one which is designed to serve as a tender, ferry, or auxiliary to another larger craft and/or a craft for first adventures in boating.
2. Is powered by paddles or one pair of oars, or a small (less than 5hp) outboard motor.
3. Has a L.O.A. not exceeding 15ft. or 5 metres.

   There will be exceptions to these guidelines, but we believe that these definitions will include 90% of all small boats and will, we hope, let you, the reader, know exactly what type of craft we have in mind.

INFLATABLE BOATS

Small inflatable boats have become extremely popular in the last twenty years. They are light, collapse for stowage, car topping and transportation, can be launched and recovered easily, will float even if swamped and are good sea boats, and when used as a tender they do not readily bump and damage the parent craft. On the other hand, they can be hard to handle in the wind, and, as they must be carefully constructed, they tend to be expensive, need careful maintenance and must have an annual service.

TENDERS

A yacht tender can be either a small inflatable, or a wood, fibreglass or metal dinghy. Inflatables do not tow well and should be secure aboard when under way.

PRAMS

A pram is a small tender with a flat bow, usually of wood or glassfibre. Their buoyancy is sometimes questionable, even with the use of buoyancy bags, which of course tend to reduce their main benefit, which is that they can transport a lot of stores from beach to boat. They can easily carry up to 3 people and are widely used.

DINGHIES

A dinghy will be of wood or GRP, and is distinguished by having a pointed bow, a transom or flat stern, two rowing thwarts, and it can carry 3–6 people, depending on size. A dinghy has a pointed stem, while a pram has a smaller "transom" at the bow. A dinghy should be able to venture out in sheltered estuary waters.

All the above craft can be propelled by oars, paddles or outboard motors.

ROWING BOATS AND SKIFFS

These can be used as pleasure, or ferry craft. They are usually larger than dinghies and have less freeboard; they can be up to 17ft. in length, and are usually propelled by two oarsmen, or for short distances even by a single scull over the transom. They are popular on lakes, rivers and sheltered estuaries, but are not for the open sea or a strong tideway.

LAUNCHES AND FISHING CRAFT

A launch is a small craft with an inboard engine. Into this category come many boats used by rod-fishermen, who also frequently use small boats with outboard engines.

RUNABOUTS AND SPORTS-BOATS

Often inflatables, these can be used for water skiing, or as tenders for sub-aqua divers.

CONSTRUCTION (MATERIALS)

Inflatable craft are made from a fabric coated, inside and out, with a rubber compound. Heavy-duty nylon is usually the basic material, coated with neoprene, or a neoprene blend.

Fibreglass (GRP) craft are increasingly popular and much cheaper than the same design in the more traditional wood or ply. Fibreglass is resistant to wear, easy to maintain, and stands hard handling. Fibreglass craft need to have buoyancy added, in the shape of sealed compartments, or inflatable bags, as unlike wood, GRP has no inherent buoyancy.

Wooden craft are traditional, expensive, require regular painting, varnishing and maintenance, are heavy but usually very strong. They also still require buoyancy bags or sealed compartments to be really safe. Plywood boats need to be constructed from top quality marine ply, and again, with buoyancy compartments.

Metal boats, in aluminium, are also available, but have no real

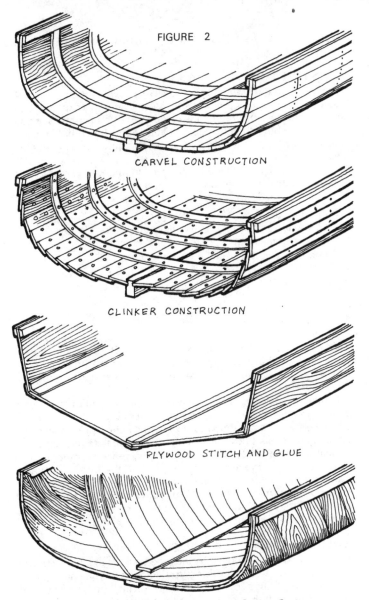

FIGURE 2

CARVEL CONSTRUCTION

CLINKER CONSTRUCTION

PLYWOOD STITCH AND GLUE

HOT MOULDED PLYWOOD OR VENEER.

11

advantages over fibreglass, except that you can knock out the dents easily.

CONSTRUCTION (METHODS)

Methods of construction include *carvel*, in which the planks are fastened edge to edge; *clinker*, where the planks overlap; plywood craft are designed in ways to utilize its strength, such as *hard chine* where the ply is joined at an angle (or chine) on each side, to form the hull. In *double chine* there are two angles instead of one.

Hulls can also be cold moulded, or hot moulded, and many craft originally constructed in ply are now available also in GRP.

WHAT TO BUY

Before you buy, sit down and list *all* the uses to which you intend to put your small boat. This list might include:

1. Tender to yacht.
2. Fishing.
3. Scuba diving.
4. As a life raft.
5. As a plaything for the children.
6. Water skiing.
7. Sailing craft.

Then decide *where* you want to use it. Conditions vary immensely and a boat suitable for fishing or water skiing on a lake or reservoir, might be quite unsuitable as a yacht tender on a tidal estuary.

Study the yachting and small boat magazines, editorial articles as well as advertisements, and send off for brochures. Visit yacht chandlers and local showrooms to study the craft, talk to the salesmen, or talk to the principals of any local sailing school.

Visit the area of your proposed activity, see what other people are using there and ask questions. Talk to the local fishermen, Coastguard or Harbour Master. Get good advice. It is always cheap. An incorrect craft is not only going to cost you hundreds of pounds, it may cost you your life. At best you may have to re-sell it, at a loss, to get the craft you *really* need.

RULES AND REGULATIONS

Rules, unlike regulations, may lack the backing of a legal statute, but a 'good rule' is something you disobey at your peril, and if there are any "rules" or regulations governing the type, or size, of craft you use, then it makes good sense to obey them.

LENGTH

Remember that piece of paper with all the relevant facts concerning the craft you want and where you can use it.

A boat of less than 10ft. L.O.A., will be very cramped with, say, a couple and two children aboard, especially with a pile of stores. Something over 12ft. will seem much larger than the actual extra 2ft. might indicate. If you need a 13'13" craft, but can only afford a 10ft one, wait until you *can* afford the 13'3" one. You need a boat with spare capacity, not one which is too small to begin with.

As a *working guide,* you need the following:

Minimum LOA	No. Aboard	
	At Sea	In Sheltered Waters
10'	Don't go to sea	2
12'	2	3
14'	3	4
16'	4	5

For rough water or when carrying stores, leave one person ashore and make another trip.

INSURANCE

Having bought your craft, have it insured. Small craft disappear for their moorings at an alarming rate, either through faulty ropework or by theft. Insurance for the craft, against ALL RISKS and at REPLACEMENT value is the very minimum cover you should carry.

Now that you have purchased a suitable craft, let us get it properly equipped.

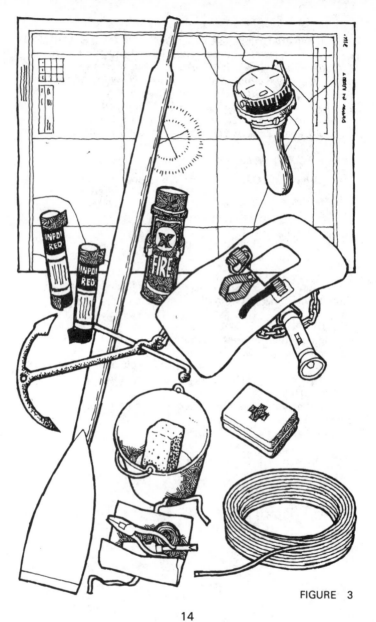

FIGURE 3

Chapter 2

EQUIPMENT

Apart from the engine, and those stores, spares and fuel which go with it, which we shall discuss later, all small boats need some additional equipment.

It depends on the boat and the area and conditions under which you use it, but a comprehensive list for open tidal waters would certainly include the following:

1. Anchor(s) and short chain and warp.
2. Bailer and sponge, or bilge pump.
3. Boat hook.
4. Chart and compass.
5. Distress flares.
6. Oars/paddles.
7. Mooring lines and spare line.
8. Fire Extinguisher.
9. An approved life-jacket or buoyancy aid for everyone on board.
10. Torch.
11. First Aid Kit.
12. Tool Kit.

This equipment must be secured on board and you must know how to use it, and realize the necessity of keeping some of it *dry*.

1. ANCHOR(S)

Boats are better off with two anchors, but any boat putting out without at least one, is sailing without an essential piece of equipment.

Small boat anchors come in various types, but suitable models for small boats are the Danforth, the CQR (Chatham Quick Release) or the 'Fishermans' anchor.

The anchor warp, or cable, should not be attached directly to the anchor stock, but secure to it by at least two metres of chain, and you need sufficient cable for any reasonable depth, say 50 metres.

You will need to put cable equivalent to three times the depth, over the side when anchoring. In 2 metres of water (6'6") you must put 6 metres (19'6") of cable over the side.

It is important to get an anchor which is large enough to hold the boat. As a rough guide, an anchor should be equal in weight

15

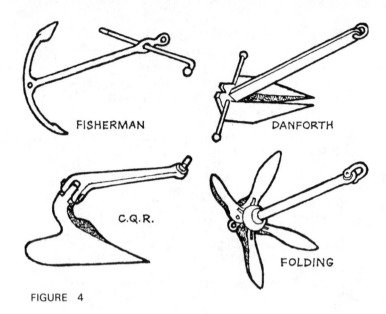

FISHERMAN   DANFORTH

C.Q.R.   FOLDING

FIGURE   4

to the length of the boat. A 20lb. anchor should hold a 20ft. boat. This is a *rough* guide and you should err on the heavy side, although some anchors dig in extra well and can be proportionately lighter. Secure the anchor(s) in the boat and coil the chain and warp down neatly.

2. BAILER, SPONGE AND BILGE PUMP

Even in light winds, some spray always comes on board, so always carry a bucket and a sponge, secured on board with line. A loose bailer will float away if you get swamped. A bucket will quickly scoop gallons of water back where it belongs, and a sponge can mop up the corners and get the boat dry again. A bilge pump is standard in some craft, and a hand pump can get into the deep recesses.

3. BOAT HOOK

Boats carry a boat hook for the simple reason that they are very useful. They come in handy for picking up a mooring, for holding onto wharf or lock chains, and for lots of other tasks. Buy one.

4. CHART AND COMPASS

A surprising number of small boats put out without a chart. A chart is simply a map and if you get lost it can help you locate your position and find your way into safe waters and home again. The *Spurbook of Chart and Compass* will tell you how to read a chart. A waterproof chart cover is a great asset. On a small boat the compass is an all-too-frequently forgotten item. A mist can clamp down suddenly offshore, and a compass is an essential item of safety equipment. Small compasses are widely available, at moderate cost, and should be secured on board away from electrical equipment and metal objects. They should be 'swung' so that the deviation on each heading can be calculated, and a true course laid. See *'Chart & Compass'*.

5. DISTRESS FLARES

Certain countries have regulations concerning flares which must be carried. As a basic guide, red flares are for distress, and white flares are position markers, used to avert a collision.

Some distress flares are hand-held, while others fire a flare into the air. Current recommendations for small craft are:

Inshore: 2 red handflares
                2 orange smoke flares.

Coastal: 4 2-star red signal flares
                4 red handflares
                2 orange smoke flares.

Offshore: 4 red parachute flares
                4 red handflares
                2 buoyant orange flares.

Collision: 4 white handflares.

Keep flares somewhere dry, but handy. Read the instructions for use NOW. Replace them if they show signs of deterioration and anyway every three years.

6. OARS AND PADDLES

Every boat should have at least two methods of propulsion. If you have sails or a motor, you carry oars as well in case a halyard jams or the motor stops. If you are under oars, you carry paddles in case you lose an oar or break one. If you *don't* carry paddles, you should have a rowlock hole or groove cut in the transom, so that if one oar is lost, you can scull over the stern with the remaining one (see chapter 4).

7. MOORING LINE (PAINTER) AND SPARE LINE

The painter will normally be used to secure the boat to a dock or jetty. On the beach you may haul the boat up and lay out the anchor over the bow to prevent it floating off, or conversely, use it to anchor the boat offshore. However you secure the boat, spare line is useful and a 50 metre coil of mooring line is a handy piece of equipment, especially if secured on a drum.

8. FIRE EXTINGUISHER

Every boat should carry a fire extinguisher. Even if you usually have no engine or fuel aboard you may one day decide to carry a petrol or gas stove for cooking lunch, and accidents can still happen, even on other craft. A 3lb (1.5 kilo) dry powder extinguisher is recommended for small boats.

9. LIFE-JACKET/BUOYANCY AID

The essential difference between the two is that a life-jacket will keep the person in the water afloat, head upright, when unconscious, while the buoyancy aid needs help from a conscious swimmer. Life-jackets or aids must be of the appropriate standard.

FIGURE 5

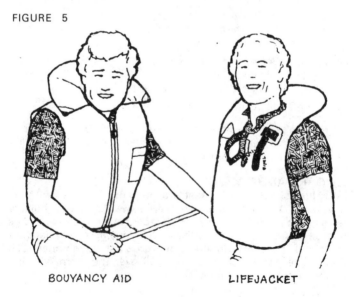

BOUYANCY AID   LIFEJACKET

Make it a 'rule' that, before entering the boat, life-jackets must be on *and secured*. An unfastened life-jacket will simply float off the person in the water. Life-jackets must not be stowed under a hatch or stuffed in a corner. They must be worn *by everyone* at all times. Make it a rule, before entering the boat, to have *all life-jackets on and secured*. Do this all the time, every time, and it will become a habit.

10. TORCH

A good torch is a useful item at any time, but very handy indeed on a small boat, It can help you to find objects lost in the bilges, serve to signal another boat, to grope your way inshore after dark, to read chart or compass. It can be hoisted on a mast or oar to serve as a riding light if you anchor.

Damp is a fearsome enemy of torch parts and batteries, so keep the torch dry and carry spare bulbs and batteries in a plastic container.

11. FIRST-AID KIT

A small first-aid kit is a useful item of equipment. A few bandages and plasters, a pair of tweezers, scissors, and an antiseptic cream is the very minimum. As with everything else, you must know how to use it. (See *Outdoor First Aid*, Spur Venture Guide).

12. TOOL KIT

A pair of pliers, plug spanner, screwdriver, assorted engine parts, insulating tape and wire, will all prove useful.

This list of basic small boat stores can be amplified as much as reason dictates and space allows. We will discuss how some of these items — oars, chart and compass etc., should be used, in subsequent chapters.

Chapter 3

OUTBOARD ENGINES

An increasing number of small craft are propelled by engines and usually engines of the outboard type. With an inboard engined craft, the two are designed together, so the engine choice is usually made for you by the designer or builder and we will only consider outboards here.

When buying your small boat, it is important to decide on your method of propulsion and if you opt for an outboard, you must be certain that the boat has a suitable transom and will perform safely and efficiently under power. You must obtain the relevant instruction manual for the engine you are going to use, and study it first before you start the engine.

ENGINE SIZE (INFLATABLES)

The all-inflated type of boat should be equipped with an engine bracket which usually consists of a step-like kit slotted into rubber brackets. A craft with an inflatable keel is obviously not as rigid as a wooden or fibreglass transom and may warp if the recommended speed is exceeded. Boats of this type for 5–12 ft. L.O.A. are usually rated for engines of between 2½ and 6hp. The propeller shaft can be long or short, and this again depends on the craft.

Average inflatable boat sizes in popular use range from 8 to 18ft. L.O.A. and the recommended engine h.p. ranges from 3hp single screw to 45hp twin screw, depending on design.

If we take three popular and established makes, we find that for their 12 to 13ft. L.O.A. range, the recommended engine size varies considerably.

AVON 12.6	S.300	30hp	Maximum
12.6	S.400	45hp	Maximum
BOMBARD 12.6		40hp	Maximum
CAMPARI 12.3 Corsair		25hp	Maximum
ZODIAC 12.6 M2 Compact		40hp	Maximum
DUNLOP 12.0 C120		25hp	Maximum

Note the 'maximum'. These are big engines and these inflatables are semi-rigid, with engines suitable for water skiing, fitted with floorboards and a keel tube, and will plane at speed when lightly laden at the bow.

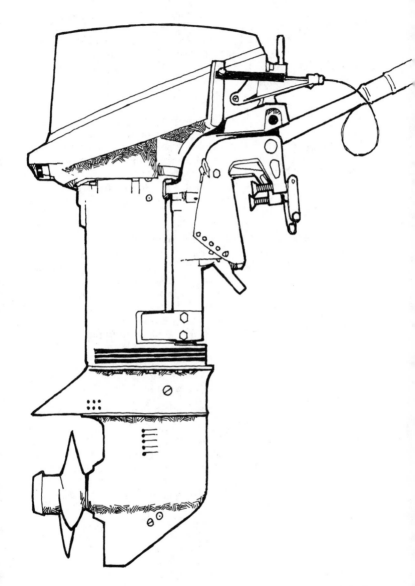

FIGURE 6

BUYING AN ENGINE

There is now a vast range of engines available. You must shop around, and talk to the widest possible number of chandlers and shops which specialise in outboard. When you have narrowed the choice, talk to current users.

MAINTENANCE

Engines will run better and last longer if they have correct and regular maintenance. If you are mechanically minded, you can do much of this yourself, and the basic checks can be done by just following the advice in the instruction manual. Out of season, the engine should be put in for an annual check, and for winterizing. It is especially important to care for the spark plugs, and carry spare ones. It is unwise to let anyone else handle your engine, as this invariably causes it to give trouble thereafter.

PROBLEMS AND TROUBLE SHOOTING

There is no end to the problems which can occur, but regular maintenance and protecting the engine from the elements when not in use will go a long way towards ensuring that the engine starts when you want it to and will not let you down at just the wrong moment.

If trouble *does* occur, you can usually solve it by analysing the fault and proceeding, step by step, towards elimination of the possible cause, referring constantly to the manual.

Problem

1. Engine won't start, or peters out.

Check Cause

1. No fuel
2. Fuel tap shut
3. Engine not primed or choke in (if applicable)
4. Engine flooded
5. Air lock in tank or fuel lines
6. Dirt or water in tank or fuel lines
7. Mixture too rich (engine smokes)
8. Plug lead(s) loose or 'shorting'
9. Magneto or condenser weak
10. Plug points dirty or badly gapped

	11. Gaskets blown
	12. Plug(s) dirty, oiled or badly gapped

Spark plugs can be heated with a lighter or blow-torch if the engine won't start, and spare plugs are unavailable. A warmed plug will often do the trick.

2. Engine will not run in neutral.	1. Check idling device 2. Check plug(s) 3. Check gaskets 4. Check if prop. shaft too deep
3. Heavy engine vibration.	1. Damaged or fouled prop. 2. Transom clamp or bracket loose 3. Carburetor over advanced 4. Plug not firing
4. Propellor fails to turn.	1. Shear pin broken 2. Prop. shaft, drive or propellor broken (or missing)
5. Prop. turns, but boat sluggish.	1. Prop. fouled 2. Prop. bent 3. Prop. too shallow.
6. Engine slows, loses power or stops.	1. Out of fuel 2. Mixture too lean 3. Mixture too rich 4. Plugs foul 5. Fuel blockage 6. Petrol/oil mixture incorrect.
7. Engine Overheating.	1. Poor petrol/oil mix. (needs more oil) 2. Cooling system or pumps U/S (air or water) 3. Intakes blocked 4. Blown gasket 5. Prop. too shallow in the water.
8. Engine 'knocks'	1. Incorrect Fuel or mix 2. Prop. or flywheel loose 3. 'Head' or cylinders need decoke 4. Overheated motor 5. Worn parts 6. Spark advanced too far

9. Engine seizes.	1. No lubrication or oil
	2. Prop. fouled
	3. Bent prop. or shaft
	4. Poor petrol/oil mix
	5. Cylinders fouled

This will take you through a range of problems from the engine failing to start to its stopping with a thud. The range of outboards and their complexity is such that we cannot go into any one engine in detail and the rules for having an engine which works when you need it are relatively simple.

1. Have a suitable engine for your craft.
2. Carry out regular maintenance, including cleaning.
3. Have it serviced regularly.
4. Know the basic causes of the more common problems and how to tackle them.
5. Carry sufficient tools and spares on board.
6. Have an alternative means of propulsion, oars, paddles, sails etc.

Everyone eventually learns to handle the eccentricities of their own engine, but a course in engine maintenance is worth attending, if available.

Chapter 4

BOAT HANDLING UNDER OARS

However you propel your small boat, you must first get on board and load it with any kit or stores. Before you go even this far, you should ring the weather service and check that the weather, tide or current conditions are such that you may safely launch and go out.

BOARDING
Adopt a routine, and follow it until it becomes an ingrained habit. A recommended routine might include the following steps:
1. Check the boat is dry and all 'bungs' are in.
2. Look at weather, sky, tide or current.
3. Check stores and equipment are all to hand and correct.
4. Everyone, including yourself, puts on a life-jacket.
5. Launch boat carefully, and/or put someone aboard.
6. Load equipment.
7. Load stores.
8. Load passengers, (step into the middle not onto the gunwales!) and trim the boat.
9. Final check round, bailer, rowlocks, etc., all correct?
10. Shove off.

LOADING
A great many small craft founder because they are overloaded, with stores or people, for the size of the boat and/or *for the conditions* they are in. It is one thing rowing ashore in a tender on a calm evening with two children and a dog, and quite another on a blustering day with a fair lop on the water, and two adults, three crates of empty bottles and a flat 12-volt battery on board — I speak of what I know! It is even more different returning at midnight when both passengers and battery are all fully charged!

The aim of correct loading is to maintain an even fore, aft and lateral trim. Ideally the boat should not be down by head or stern, or canted to one side. If it lists to port it will tend to steer to starboard!

If you have three people in the boat and one rowing, put one in the bow and one in the stern, and distribute any stores to keep the boat even and maintain a fair freeboard.

When powered by an outboard, the bow will tend to lift anyway, but do not for this reason load the boat for a bow-heavy trim, or the bow will dig under when the engine slows or stops. Conversely, a bow-light inflatable, trimmed by the stern exposes a lot of bow to wind and sea and this can be caught by a gust or wave and the boat turned over.

If your small boat can hold five under ideal conditions, reduce the number drastically if conditions are less than ideal. In the rough waters caused by wind-against-tide conditions, reduce the total numbers intended abroad by 40% or even more. It is much better to row some out and come back for the others than have all floundering around the harbour or being swept away by the current. The same holds good for stores; reduce the load and make another trip.

Because there are so many types of small boats it is impossible to be specific, but here again there are some working rules.

Length of Craft	Number Abroad	Max. Load
10ft.	2	400lbs.
12ft.	3	550lbs.
14ft.	4	740lbs.

These are *suggested* loadings for *fair* conditions. As conditions worsen, take people or stores out. Note the weights again. If you have a 10ft. boat, and two hefty, 168lbs people aboard (2 x 168lbs = 336lbs.) you can at a *maximum* on a *good day* carry 64lbs. of stores. If you think metric, 2.21lbs. = 1 kilo and 3ft. 3ins. = 1 metre.

These working rules can only be a guide. Inflatable craft can patently carry more and unstable fibreglass praams much less. Just remember:
1. The majority of swampings are caused by overloading.
2. Don't forget the weather and water conditions.
3. Trim the boat evenly and allow a more than adequate freeboard.

SHOVING OFF

The moment you cast off the painter is always a tricky one. If you are close to the jetty, or being pushed off a beach, you may be unable to give a good pull on the oars until you are well clear. Off a beach, someone has to get their feet wet, and push the boat out, bows to sea.

Leave with your bow into the tide or current. If you are alongside a jetty, you can often get away by using 'springs' to sweep the bow out and get the oars in before you cast off the stern line, or vice-versa. You can also use paddles, or your boat hook to gain clearance. Once away, coil down the painter, ready for use, but above all, have a routine, and don't flounder about.

BOAT RULES

A few 'rules' for the people aboard are useful. These ought to be commonsense, but as this is rather uncommon please note:

1. Board and leave by stepping into or from the middle of the boat, not on the sides (gunwales).
2. No one stands up in the boat.
3. No 'skylarking' or unnecessary movement.
4. All hands inside the boat — crushed fingers are no fun.
5. Life-jackets to be worn before boarding and fastened at all times.

ROWING

Of one person has both oars, he is *sculling.* If two or more people have an oar each, they are *rowing.* Rowing, other than for a few quick arm strokes for manoeuvring is an activity powered by the back and legs. The oarsman should sit squarely in the middle of the thwart. His feet should be planted firmly on the floorboards, heels together, or braced against a 'stretcher' or under another thwart, if possible. Then, in the event of a miss-stroke, or 'catching a crab' he may not tumble backwards, off his thwart and upset the boat.

FIGURE 7

The oar should be grasped firmly, the hands four to six inches apart, elbows close to the sides and the wrists raised.

To row, the rower leans forward, arms straight and lowers the blade into the water by raising the hands. He then pulls back on the 'loom', keeping the arms and body straight, leaning backwards until the back is past the upright position. The stroke is completed by bending the elbows and pulling the loom into the chest, the blade clearing the water. To restart the sequence, on the return, the oar blade is feathered, the wrists being dropped to turn the blade horizontally to the water. At sea, a short chopping stroke will be more effective than a long pull.

Good rowing takes practice and can be a graceful and rhythmic action, powering the boat forward without the craft losing way.

The sensible small boat owner will practise rowing until he is really proficient and has included in his rowing skills such techniques as pulling with one and two oars, 'backing' the boat by pushing on the loom rather than pulling, and turning the boat by backing with one oar and pulling with the other, as well as such manoeuvres as leaving the shore, coming alongside on either hand, casting-off, shipping your oars, placing them in the rowlocks, and bringing them inboard. An inflatable is high exposed to the wind and can be hard to row in a breeze so these are usually better propelled with paddles.

SINGLE OAR SCULLING

If you lose an oar, what do you do? You can be glad you have a paddle, or using your remaining oar, paddle with it over the side. If you sit well over, to heel the boat, and the oar is not too long, then you may manage like this, but all oarsmen should learn to "scull" with one oar over the stern. To do this you will need a rowlock hole drilled in the transom, into which you can plug your rowlock, or a rowlock notch. In some countries, such as France, such a notch is compulsory by law. If you have neglected this precaution, make a rope grommet and slip this over the oar, and secure carefully at the transom.

Study the diagram and practise next time you have your boat out. The knack is to use short chopping strokes, at an angle *from* the fore-and-aft line of the boat, which will keep the boat travelling in a straight line. Carve the oar across the stern in an 'S' or Figure-of-eight shaped sweep, twisting the blade to set it for the return at the end of each sweep. The angle of the oar over the stern should be at about 45°.

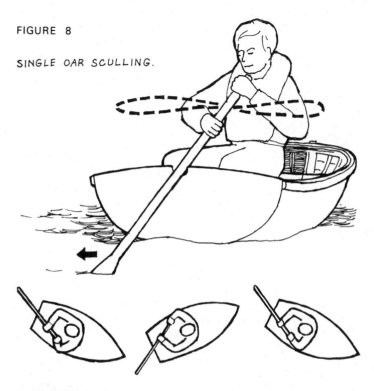

FIGURE 8

SINGLE OAR SCULLING.

PADDLING

Paddling is much harder than rowing since more of the effort has to be made with the arms and shoulders. On the other hand, you can see where you are going and a paddled craft is easier to manoeuvre in a confined space.

COMING ALONGSIDE

If you are crossing tidal waters, head upstream of your destination and 'crab' across stream, letting your craft drift down to your landing point bow into the current before you row into the current and come alongside. If you try and come alongside with the current you will come in fast and out of control.

Always come alongside heading into the current, the tide, or, if that is the dominant factor, the wind. You will have much greater control. You can go well forward from your landing or boarding point and drop back to it, bringing your boat alongside with a few short strokes with the offside oar. If you miss your landing point, or are too far to get a firm hold on chain or ladder, don't make grabs for it. Pull away and come in again.

GETTING ASHORE OR ON BOARD

Once alongside, let the bowman board or land first, taking the painter and securing the boat firmly before assisting the passengers to disembark. Get at least one adult aboard the yacht or ashore, before the children, so that they are never without help. Then unload the stores, the boat equipment, including the oars and paddles. Then secure the boat, put out fenders, doubling up on the lines, checking the security of hatch clips and covers, and finally, the oarsman boards. Never step on the gunwhale, always step out from the middle of the boat.

BEACH LANDINGS

Unless there is surf on the shore, come in bows first with someone ready to go over the bows with the painter. This person, the 'bowman', will hold the boat on, until the rest get ashore, and the lightened boat can be manhandled ashore. This can be the time when most damage is done to the craft. Do not let the craft pound on the shore, or drag it over the pebbles unless the bottom is supported with rubbing strakes.

If there is surf on the beach, it is best to stay out of it or come in by anchoring offshore and letting the craft drift in, paying out line over the bow.

The secret of all good boat handling is good technique and lots of practice.

Chapter 5

BOAT HANDLING UNDER POWER

In an increasingly mechanical age it is inevitable that more and more boats are being powered by engines. This is fine, providing oars, paddles (or a spare engine) are carried as well; this is why we learn to handle the boat under oars in preference to power first.

BOARDING
While the need for a routine is as important with a power boat as well as with oars, parts of the routine are necessarily different. You might adopt the following procedure:

1. Check on weather, tide and current. Life-jackets on.
2. Check all stores and equipment.
3. Check all tubes and compartments inflated and sealed.
4. Launch boat, secure and load stores.
5. Fit engine to brackets, and secure with rope or chain.
6. Check if fuel tanks adequately full. Spare fuel and oil aboard?
7. Prime and start engine. Allow to idle.
8. Embark passengers and trim the boat.
9. Final check round.
10. Cast off, recover ropes, coil painter, beware of fouling propeller.

Your list of stores should now include engine spares and tools.

SHOVING OFF
Not all outboards have a reverse, and it may be necessary to paddle away from the jetty or the clutter of other craft, before shipping the paddles and engaging the motor. Check the motor will start before you do this.

Most propellers turn clockwise, if viewed from astern. This has the tendency to turn the boat stern to starboard when the propeller is going ahead and to port when going astern. With practice this feature can be used to manoeuvre the boat, by short engine bursts, out of a confined space.

It is important to remember that a boat is manoeuvred by swinging the *stern.* Many people believe that a powerboat, particularly if equipped with a wheel, can be handled like a car, and may even imagine that a boat has brakes! If you swing the bow out hard to leave the jetty, you will inevitably thump the stern or quarter against the stone, a steel post, or the thin fibreglass

FIGURE 9

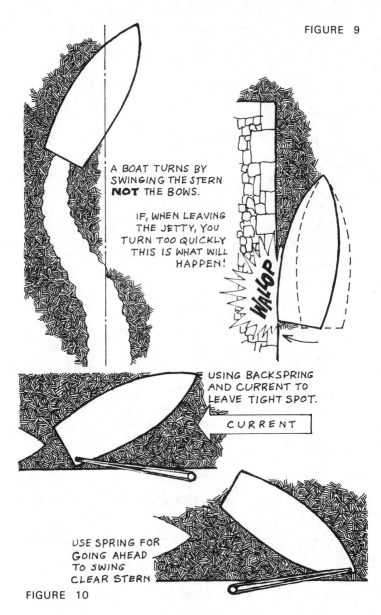

A BOAT TURNS BY SWINGING THE STERN **NOT** THE BOWS.

IF, WHEN LEAVING THE JETTY, YOU TURN TOO QUICKLY THIS IS WHAT WILL HAPPEN!

WALLOP

USING BACKSPRING AND CURRENT TO LEAVE TIGHT SPOT.

CURRENT

USE SPRING FOR GOING AHEAD TO SWING CLEAR STERN

FIGURE 10

hull of your yacht. Ease away, into the current, and fend off carefully.

If using 'springs', be sure the cast-off ropes are kept well clear of the prop. Do not put the prop. deep in the water until you are sure you have sufficient depth. If it strikes the bottom there may be a nasty clang, a broken sheer-pin, or, even worse, a bent blade or shaft.

CAVITATION

Cavitation is a situation in which the propeller spins at speed without increasing the speed of the craft. If the prop speed employed is too fast for the shape or size of the propeller, the pressure of air and water is insufficient to supply solid water to the blades. The sensation felt aboard is one of a high revving engine, but without any gain in speed. It is very necessary to have the correct propeller for your particular engine.

THE RUDDER

With outboards, the engine itself is turned to steer the boat.

Other craft have rudders and it is necessary to appreciate that the effect of the rudder is multiplied by the speed of the boat. If the boat is at speed, a very small movement of the tiller will have a dramatic effect on the boat. Violent tiller/rudder movements are to be avoided at speed, and the helmsman should be prepared to throttle back before making any sharp turn.

There is a limit to the effective amount a helm can be put over. The maximum is about 35° on either side of the 'midships' position. Beyond this the rudder will simply act as a drag and kick hard.

Rudders can be damaged by ill use or collision, just as props. can, although most rudders are now held down by shock-cord, and will rise if they hit an obstacle. Rudder fittings need attention and maintenance for the loss of the rudder can cause problems.

HANDLING UNDER POWER

The effective speed generated by an outboard will largely depend on the loading of the boat. An unladen inflatable can go like the wind with quite a small engine. The 9ft. Avon, with a 5hp. Yamaha can get up to 15 knots. Put two people on board and this drops down by 50% and the freeload is also much reduced. A 'spray-dodger' in the bow is a great help in keeping the boat dry. Don't put too much weight forward for it will make the bow dig in. Trim the boat and if you have a long trip to your destination it is a good idea to take the boat out and make one quick circle, with a burst at full power, before returning to pick up your passengers. This may reveal any problems, which you can remedy before you leave again, and avoid a breakdown in open waters.

COMING ALONGSIDE

If you can handle a boat skilfully under oars, you will find it easier, if faster, under power. The same techniques apply, but when coming alongside be ready to fend off. Have a bowman ready, and, if you have enough people aboard have someone ready with a sternline as well. Once you have them ashore or on board the yacht be sure they have tied the craft up correctly. (See Knots p. 39).

FIGURE 11

DON'T DO THIS!

WINDAGE

Inflatables are light, shallow craft, and expose a high side to the wind. At low speeds especially, this can push the craft about quite a bit, and it will take experience to recognise the effect of wind and cope with it.

Small boat handling is a skill, and like all skills, it grows with experience and is maintained by practise.

Chapter 6

BASIC SEAMANSHIP

Not all small boats can or should be used on tidal waters and,
unless they are designed for such use, they should not be taken
out to sea.

'Thy sea is so great and my boat is so small.' Being closer to the
elements the small boat sailor needs an even better grasp of boat
handling and the skills which make the seaman. In the Royal
Navy they say that a ship is judged by its boats, and the way a
yachtsman handles his tender is a good guide to the way he sails
his yacht. Here are just a few basic considerations for the small
boat sailor to think about.

THE ELEMENTS
Small boats are governed by and must bow to, the elements.
Wind can make even a short trip in a small boat impossible, very
long, or extremely hard work. Currents and tidal streams can take
complete control over a small craft, which lacks the power to
stem them.

You may appear to be moving ahead or stemming the current,
while actually being carried downstream. It is worth
remembering that currents are usually less strong inshore, and
on the inside of bends. Strong currents can prolong your trip
considerably so that your engine requires more fuel. These are
just a few considerations, which may occur before the conditions
worsen noticeably and create more obvious problems.

ROLLING AND PITCHING
A boat is *rolling* when waves approach from the beam and cause
the boat to lean alternatively to port and starboard. Having
sufficient freeboard is a comfort at such a time.

Rolling is not in itself dangerous, but can increase until the
boat is shipping water. So reduce rolling by directing the boat
slightly into the waves.

A boat *pitches* when the bow rises to the waves and buries
itself in the trough. This is less serious than excessive rolling, but
the bow of a heavily-laden craft can bury itself and ship water. If
the waves are short and steep, and the boat speed excessive, the
boat may smack hard into the approaching waves, and this
pounding is hard on craft and crew, so speed should be reduced.

ROUGH SEAS

A small boat should not be out in rough seas or strong conditions, but such situations can arise, even in sheltered places, when the wind or tide changes. Always choose a sheltered route even if it is longer than the direct one, and be prepared to go ashore if the situation seems to be worsening.

Do not let your boat become broadside-on to the waves or 'broach to', for it may roll over or swamp. The boat can also be too slow for the waves and be caught under a breaking crest, *pooped,* or roll across the wave, as the bow or stern rises, presenting her beam to the water in 'a broach', when she can be swamped or rolled over.

BARS

Many estuaries and harbours have a *bar,* or shallow near the entrance. Under certain conditions of wind and tide, surf can build up in there in an alarming way. In a small boat, low in the water, such bars are difficult to see. One minute you can be in placid water and the next among waves. Local knowledge of such perils is essential, so ask the fishermen for it.

If you have to go through a bar, have all the gear tied down, be sure your best oarsman is at the oars, or that your engine is well warmed up and unlikely to stall at the crucial moment. Life-jackets should be worn at all times, so to tell you that they are essential when in rough water *should* be unnecessary.

WAVES

It is inevitable that the small boat sailor will encounter waves. If you went out only on placid days, your trips would be few indeed. Waves of moderate size, evenly spaced and unbroken, are no real danger. Unless power fails you should have no trouble. If you lose engine or oars, you may need to anchor, or use a sea-anchor to keep the boat's head to the swell.

SEA-ANCHORS

One simple emergency method is to attach a line to your bucket and fling it over the bow, having attached the line to the bow of your boat. Your boat will drift off to leeward, but the bucket will grip the water and pull your bow round into the waves. A heavy rope trailed over the stern is also effective.

Sea-anchors, made from good quality canvas, are a useful small boat store, and can be used while fishing, or when having a meal in places where the water is too deep for your normal anchor. (Fig. 12).

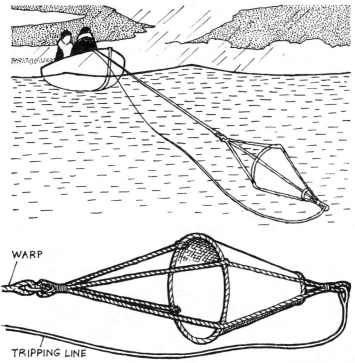

WARP

TRIPPING LINE

FIGURE 12

As a rough rule, the diameter of the larger end should be about 1" for each 1 ft. of boat length. The anchor should be streamed from the bow by a line, and lie off about three times the length of the boat. A lighter 'tripping line' should be attached to the base of the anchor, or recovery can be hard work.

If the waves are breaking around your craft, a little oil dripped over the side will reduce their effect considerably. You don't need to slosh gallons over the side, half-cupfuls at intervals will be quite effective.

SURF

In previous chapters we have assumed that most departures and arrivals in a small boat are to or from boat or jetty, but small craft are also used to ferry people on to, or from, open shores, and if waves are breaking on them, this calls for technique.

Leaving such a shore, the bow must be kept into the waves, with someone holding the bow or stern until the oarsman or engine can provide sufficient way. Someone may have to wade out, pushing the boat deeper. In surf, coming on to a beach, it is a good idea to stream the anchor over the bow and drift in low to sea paying out the warp, using power or oars to keep the boat straight.

With many inflatables, you can run under power right on to the beach, but this should not be tried in breaking waves, or the craft may swamp. If waves fill the boat, do not even attempt to lift it until it has been bailed out. Be careful not to damage the prop. or rudder when entering shallow water, shutting down power or raising the prop. early.

SWAMPING

A small boat can easily be filled by even one wave coming on board. Running before the waves sounds like the answer, but this is a practice open to error as water can easily come in over the transom.

It is best to keep the seas on the bows or quarter, and as an added security, have someone detailed to bail out continually any water which does come on board. Loose water sloshing about in the bilges can drastically reduce stability.

Many swampings are caused by that fundamental small boat error, *overloading*. It is not seamanlike to overload the craft, and you must load the craft after examining and allowing for the tide and weather.

TIDES AND CURRENTS

Once, with three companions, I had to leave a yacht moored on a 'trot' about half a mile offshore. We launched the tender, which drummed madly at the end of the painter, climbed in, detailed our best oarsman to put us ashore near the pub and cast off. Mick bent to the oars and rowed, and rowed, and rowed! Sweat burst on his brow. After several minutes we had advanced from the quarter to the mainmast shrouds. With a final gasp, Mick heaved mightily on the offside oar, laid us alongside the yacht and clung desperately to the rail. It was simply not possible to row against that current, and we sat aboard for two more hours until slack water.

Always allow for the effect of strong tides. You may not be able to make it across them safely. Sometimes you can wait, but if you have a train to catch, or want to get out on the flood, you may be tempted to go in unsuitable conditions. Had we tipped over — and

Mick catching a crab would have done it, that tide would have swept us away in the night. Would a drink have been worth it?

Changing oarsmen is always a tricky moment. No one should stand in the boat, and if you have to change oarsmen, stay low, stay smooth and move together.

KNOTS

A good seaman, or anyone skilled in small boats should know and use a few good knots; you will find all the knots you will ever need in the *Spur Book of Knots* (which includes whipping and splicing).

However, for servicing your boat, the following knots are useful:

1. Bowline.
2. Sheet bend.
3. Fisherman's or Anchor Bend.
4. Reef Knot.
5. Tugboat Hitch.
6. Clove Hitch.
7. Figure-of-Eight Knot.

FIGURE 13

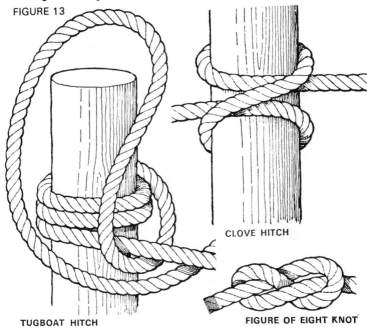

CLOVE HITCH

TUGBOAT HITCH

FIGURE OF EIGHT KNOT

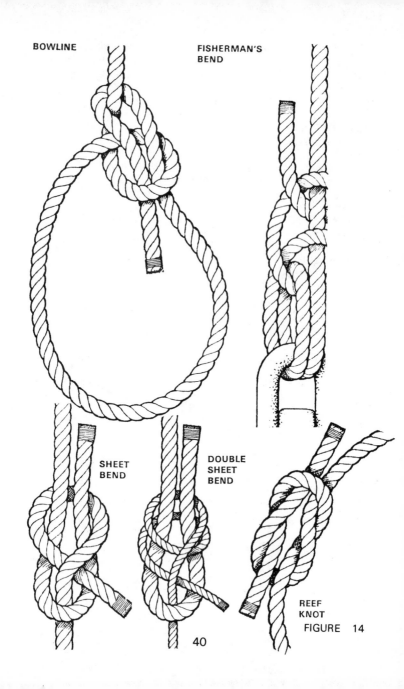

BOWLINE

FISHERMAN'S BEND

SHEET BEND

DOUBLE SHEET BEND

REEF KNOT

FIGURE 14

40

Chapter 7

INLAND WATERS

Good boat handling skills are not just necessary at sea, or even on salt water. Rivers, lakes and canals all have their own requirements and special problems.

Whereas inland waters do not have the problems associated with tides, they do however have their own particular requirements, such as strong river currents, narrow manoeuvring space, and so on.

Our rivers system has well defined limits for tidal waters such as Teddington Lock on the Thames and the fresh water areas of rivers are by and large far easier to work than tidal regions.

In addition to rivers there is a vast network of canals throughout the U.K. To own one's own boat on a canal is not usually very satisfactory, as the range for exploration either way up the canal is limited. Mooring in rivers and canals is simpler than for tidal reaches as no allowances need be made.

You may come across movable bridges on our canals, usually pretty self-evident as to how they are used. Be sure to allow for the slope of the underside of the bridge as you go through. If you intend using any of the tunnels make sure you have a powerful torch. If yo can see another boat coming, wait. Wear something waterproof to stop the drips from the tunnel roof soaking you.

One very common mistake made by inexperienced users on canals is for the bowman to leap ashore with his painter and pull the bows in strongly. This has the effect of pushing out the stern. All that is needed is for someone to just hold the bows in position.

LICENSING

One problem which usually exists is the problem of licences. Small boats on open waters are usually, but not invariably, free from the need for a licence, unless they carry passengers for hire or reward, or have to comply with local byelaws on safety. On inland waters and most estuaries, a licence is usually required, while certain countries, France being one good example, insist that people handling larger craft or powered craft over a certain h.p. have had instruction and possess the necessary certificate.

So, if using your boat on any inland water, check the licensing requirements for your craft and yourself.

FIGURE 15

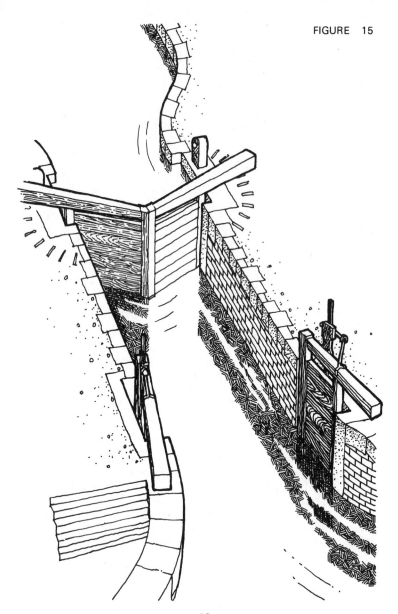

42

LOCKS

Locks appear on many rivers and canals and repay prior investigation. Some locks have boat-rollers, which small craft can use to bypass the lock and so avoid lock charges, but locks exist for two purposes:

1. To control the level of water in the 'cut' — the region between locks.
2. To lift boats up and down from one level to another.

All river locks are accompanied by a nearby water-chute or weir, which draws off water from the 'cut', the rate of flow on the weir and the depth in the 'cut' being controlled by sluices.

If the lock is unfamiliar, and there is no lock-keeper, it is a good idea to land and look at the lock before entering. If the lock gates are open, examine the mechanism closely and read any instructions before operating the mechanism. Life-jackets on in locks, and boathook to hand are two basic 'rules'.

Chapter 8

PILOTAGE

Small boats, of the type we have in mind would not normally go out of sight of land or even far offshore. The people on board should know at least the elements of offshore navigation and the rules which apply to small craft on crowded waters. Without this knowledge, however well you can handle your boat you are like a car driver with no knowledge of the Highway Code.

RULES OF THE ROAD (SEA)

The phrase which people recite like a good luck charm is: 'Steam — or power — gives way to sail — (or manual propulsion) but while this is generally true, it is by no means always the case, and certainly not an insurance policy. It is not much fun being legally right if you end up dead!

All craft are governed by the *Collision Regulations,* and the following points are worth noting.

1. The overtaking vessel always keeps clear of the vessel in front, even if the overtaking vessel is under sail.
2. Meeting another craft dead ahead, both give way to starboard, passing port side to port side.
3. Deep draft vessels have priority in a channel.
4. If in doubt, don't cross ahead of an oncoming vessel, you may not make it.
5. Show a light at night red (port) and green (starboard).

BUOYAGE

All harbours and estuaries will be buoyed. In some cases this consists of cans on poles or 'withies', which mark the channel, but in most anchorages there will be the full range of buoys. You will find them shown on your charts, and they will help you find your way about. So, to help read the chart you should purchase an Admiralty publication, the *Chart No. 5011.* This is actually a slim book, but it will help you read chart symbols and find your way about.

BUOYS

Buoys are used to mark navigable channels, and various kinds of dangers. They are placed in the interests of commercial shipping and this gives the first clue. A rock covered by at least 2 fathoms of water at low tide is a major hazard to almost all ships. To the

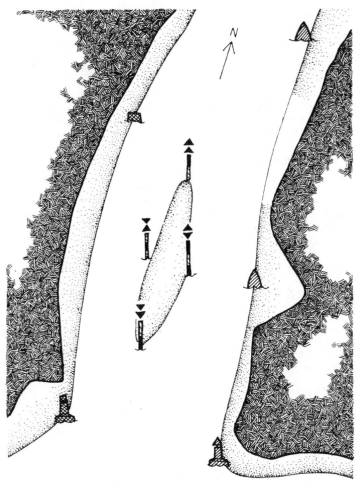

AN EXAMPLE OF I.A.L.A. SYSTEM A BUOYAGE.

FIGURE 16

RED

YELLOW

GREEN

small boat sailor the only significance is that it may cause breaking waves in bad weather. So, having checked the rock and its depth on the chart, we may, if we wish, ignore the marking buoys completely, in fair conditions.

In buoyed waters used by commercial shipping, small boats are usually safer if they stay out of the channel, unless the water outside is excessively shallow, or has steep sandbanks. The chart will show whether you may safely navigate outside the channel or not, and usually you cab. A careful study of the chart, along your plotted course, will reveal such features and possible hazards.

Some buoys can be ignored — in each case with due reference to the chart. Even those which you must watch, for example, those showing the way into a drying harbour at about half tide, will be clearly marked on the chart. The chart and the 5011 will also show you the shape and colour of buoys together with any identifying marks and day-cruising local chart and 5011 will soon teach you about them.

It is essential to understand buoyage. You can afford to take time to learn this part, but you must not neglect the opportunity to learn whenever you have the chance. The buoyance system is currently changing to the I.A.L.A. system.

I.A.L.A. SYSTEM

The main features of the standard European system are shown in Fig. 16. Channel marking buoys; red, flat topped — port-hand to left; green, conical — starboard-hand to right, are used to show the best way *into* a port, or up a river. Note carefully the *into* and *up.* It is supposed that a ship entering a harbour will be in greater need of assistance than one leaving, so the buoys are all right-way-round *when entering*. On leaving port, they appear on the opposite side.

CARDINAL SYSTEM

Dangers are marked by 'Cardinal' buoys. The important feature of which is the 'topmark', consisting of triangles which point up or down to show the direction of the danger. The illustration (Fig. 17) shows you which is which.

Buoys do have one great use for the small boat sailor. They are all identified by names or numbers, both on the chart and on the buoys, so they establish an accurate position for you.

Even in clear weather, the process of identifying buoys is very

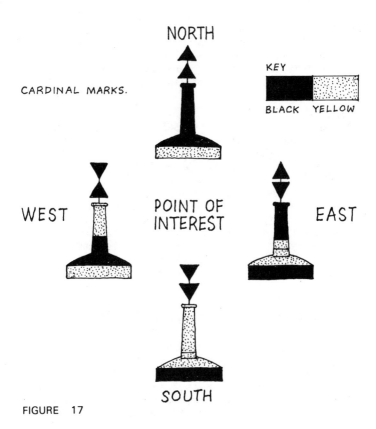

CARDINAL MARKS.

NORTH

KEY
BLACK YELLOW

WEST

POINT OF INTEREST

EAST

SOUTH

FIGURE 17

useful. It is well worth planning a cruise to pass close by as many buoys as possible, even though it may not be the most direct line to your destination. Each time you arrive at one identified buoy, you know *exactly* where you are, and this will give you great peace of mind. Never assume, though, that because a buoy is in the 'right' position, it's the 'right' buoy. Go and check, or use your binoculars!

Some marks ashore, such as 'leading marks' or lighthouses, are maintained by Trinity House, and these are always marked on charts. The best known are lighthouses, which are rarely close enough to one another to cause any confusion.

LEADING MARKS

'Leading Marks' are another type of shore marker. They consist of two posts, or pylons, usually with lights for night use, which must be kept in line to ensure that you are in a certain channel, or clear of certain rocks. The lower mark is always the one nearest to you.

WHAT IS A CHART?

A chart is a scale-drawing of the seabed and coastline, drawn to various scales and giving, by colours, marks and symbols, such information as depth, channels, buoys, and lights. They have a great deal in common with the land-based topography maps, and if you are already familiar with topo maps, you will have made a good start towards understanding charts. The most complete range of charts is produced by the British Admiralty.

The Admiralty has produced a book, although being the Admiralty it is actually called a chart — No. 5011; with it you will be able to interpret all the signs, colours and symbols on the chart.

Buy a 5011 and spend an evening or two browsing over it. It will give you all the information you need on reading a chart.

LATITUDE AND LONGITUDE

The lines which run vertically down the chart are lines of longitude. The lines which run horizontally across the chart are lines of latitude.

Latitude expresses the angular distance North or South of the Equator in degrees. Each degree is subdivided into 60 minutes, and each minute into sixty seconds. This may be very academic stuff for the small boat sailor but the chart does have useful information, and this is a part of it.

Minutes of latitude are useful: 1 minute of latitude = 1 nautical mile. You can, therefore, use the latitude scale on the side of the chart as your distance scale.

It is worth noting here that whenever you take the distance measurement off the latitude scale, you do so at a point as near as possible parallel to your position on the chart.

COMPASS ROSE

One feature not found on a topographic map is the 'compass rose'. There will be several of these compass rings on the chart, each consisting of two circles. The outer ring shows true NORTH, and the inner ring gives MAGNETIC NORTH. (Fig. 18)

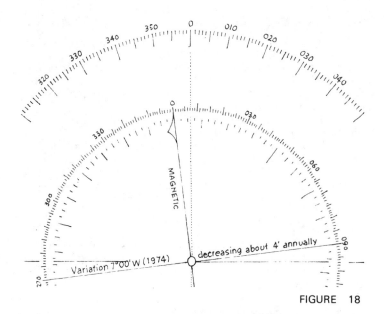

FIGURE 18

CHART SCALE

The best scale for use on small craft is 1:75000, which makes 1"
= 1 nautical mile (approx.). A nautical mile is about 6,080ft.
(approx.). Another popular scale with estuary or dinghy sailors is
1:20,000 which gives lots of detail. Note that a knot = 1 sea mile
per hour. It is a measurement of time as well as distance.

METRIC CHARTS

In recent years most Admiralty charts have gone metric. This will
not affect scale or distance, as everyone, even the French have
stuck to the existing system using MILLES for Miles and NOUEDS
for speed. It does, however, affect DEPTH, which is now
measured in metres (39") instead of the old fathoms.

One final thought. Even though non-Admiralty charts don't get
the same attention with regard to corrections, they go out of date
just as fast. We have mentioned the care necessary for installing
and checking the compass. The same meticulous attention is
necessary with charts. Keep them up to date, by noting changes
in "Notices to Mariners".

TRUE AND MAGNETIC BEARINGS: VARIATION

Within the Compass Rose, the Variation (from True to Magnetic) is noted, and the annual rate of change.

Variation is the angular difference between True North (the direction of the North Pole) and Magnetic North. The Magnetic Pole is situated somewhere to the North of Canada and to this pole all compass needles point.

The Magnetic Pole is not fixed, but moves a little each year. this annual change is shown on the 'Compass Rose'.

The variation differs according to where you are, due to the varying effect of the Magnetic Pole. Thanks to the inner (magnetic) ring on the compass rose, it is possible to do most of your calculations on magnetic, and in small boats you can stay in magnetic, as it saves time and the possibility of error.

DEVIATION

A compass needle will be attracted off its correct bearing by the magnetic attraction of metal and electrical fittings on the boat. This part of the compass error is called 'deviation' and it must be allowed for as well.

VARIATION AND DEVIATION

Two vessels, in the same spot, would, because of their different loads and fittings, have different *'deviations'* but the same *'variation'*. The same vessel in two different spots, would have the same 'deviation', but different 'variation'. Got it?

CONVERTING TRUE TO MAGNETIC AND BACK

Many small boat calculations are made in 'True' so please note that to convert a 'True' bearing to a 'Magnetic' compass one, you *add* Westerly variations and *subtract* Easterly ones.

DRYING HEIGHTS AND SOUNDINGS

You will find the chart covered with little figures like 2_1 and 6_7.

The first example, with the line underneath, indicates a drying height, i.e., an area which is above chart-datum, and the figures tell you that this is a spot which stands 2.4 metres above chart datum *at low-tide.*

All the 'soundings', like our second example, 6_7, are depths below chart datum, and, in simple terms, even at low water you will be in 6.7 metres of water. So unless your craft draws 6.8, which is unlikely in a small boat, you have no problem.

COMPASSES

for the dinghy or small boat, the main compass will be fixed inboard, and is called a 'steering compass'. Check that you can read the 'compass card' easily. The 'compass card' is the swivelling card or disc within the compass bowl, marked in degrees and/or with the 'points' of the compass NORTH (N), WEST (W), S.E., N.E., and so on. The 360° rotation is now almost universal and although you will not need, and may not be able, to steer within 5° of a given point, you must check the readability of the card (and your own eyesight).

There are, broadly speaking, two sorts of steering compass, the flat grid steering type, and the graduated card type, which can perhaps be mounted at eye level. Before buying a compass, consider your own boat. There are various ways of mounting a compass, and it is largely a matter of convenience. Hand-bearing compasses are very useful equipment in small boats, and you will find them useful for taking bearings on the shore, or measures angles on approaching ships.

ADJUSTERS

Any compass worth buying will have some device for adjusting the compass to compensate for 'deviation' caused by metal or electrical fittings in the boat. Find out where the 'adjusters' are, how they work, and be sure they will be accessible when the compass is installed. This applies to fixed mounted compasses, not to the hand-bearing type.

POINTS ON BUYING COMPASSES

Don't buy in a hurry. Buy a reputable make. They are not cheap, so buy from a ship's chandler or compass manufacturer.

INSTALLING THE COMPASS

To be effective in use, your compass must be correctly installed and placed where you can see it comfortably.

You may feel that having carried your expensive new toy back on board and wedged it in place in some handy spot, you can then embark on a 20 mile trip. If so, you are in for a nasty surprise. No compass is any use until *proved, checked and adjusted.*

INTERFERENCE

The principal thing to avoid during installation is metallic or electrical interference causing 'deviation' or distorting of the compass reading.

The biggest cause of interference is the engine, inboard or outboard; then dynamos, batteries, radios, logs, echo sounders, wiring, metal objects, anchors, shrouds.

On a rubber, wood or GRP craft the difficulties lessen to a reasonable proportion if you can maintain clearance of *3ft. or more* from the worst offenders.

STOWAGE

You may decide to install your compass while on the beach or at anchor. It's a nice job for an afternoon in early Spring. Then comes your first trip, and you load on board your spare anchor, a radio set, a sack of tinned goodies, and assorted tools — bang goes your deviation calculations, and on go more sources of interference. You must have regular places for stowage, and check your compass when the boat is, in all respects, ready for sea.

LINING UP THE COMPASS

The boat must point correctly down the desired compass course, and unless the compass is lined up exactly on or parallel to the fore and aft line of the boat, the compass will point in one direction, and you will be heading in another.

DO NOT assume that bulkheads, thwarts, lockers, etc., are either parallel or square to the keel — get out a spirit level and check. Should you detect an error, do not be surprised. Check your measurements carefully.

Once the compass is installed, it must be adjusted to minimise deviation.

DEVIATION

All compasses contain errors, and they contribute to what is described as the TOTAL COMPASS ERROR. Deviation is part of the compass error, and can be caused by many things. Interference, incorrect installation, electrical storms, or magnetic attraction, to name but a few. Two points about deviation are crucial:

1. Deviation will vary with every boat.
2. Deviation will vary with every compass heading.

You have, therefore, to know the deviation for your craft on various compass headings and the best way to do this is to prepare a deviation card.

DEVIATION CARDS

Provided you are not always moving the anchors or radios about, the deviation will probably remain constant on any particular heading. So, if you record the heading (of course) you will be able to use the information to correct the compass reading on that course heading at some future date. It is usually enough to check the deviation against the main compass points, N; N.N.W; W.N.W; etc.

You then collect this information together on a Deviation Card, giving the compass heading, and the adjustment necessary to correct it. You can give this either as a plus (+) or minus (-) or an East (E) or West (W). For example, if your desired heading was North (360°N) but your compass read 357°N) but your compass read 357°N you would need to add 3°N to get the right heading. So Magnetic Heading 0° but deviation +3°(E) Compass Heading 003°M. If you set 003° on the compass you have allowed for deviation and are heading due North.

Course	Deviation
N	2°E
NE	3°E
E	5°E
SE	2°W
S	2°W
SW	4°E
W	3°E
NW	4°E

Or like this:
Course = 167°M
Deviation
Deviation = 3°E
Compass Course = 164°C

FINAL CHECK

Once you have checked (or swung) your compass through the 16 points, there is one simple, but useful, check to make certain that you have not put in a plus instead of a minus, or added in the date!

Simply add or subtract all the corrections and divide by the number of corrections (in this case 16). The average correction ought to be zero. In any event, the error should not be more than 1°, and if it is, then the compass needs rotating slightly, or the fore and aft alignment needs checking.

Let us just summarise what we have covered on compasses:

1. Buy the best compass you can afford from a reputable stockist.
2. Consider where and how you will install it.
3. Watch out for causes of deviation.
4. Check the compass on 16 points, against some fixed reference point.
5. Prepare a deviation card.
6. Check the calculations on your deviation card.

Notice that check, check and check again is the watchword. If in any doubt, get expert help from an experienced friend, or get professional advice.

If your small boat is used only as a yacht tender, for ferrying stores and crew between ship and shore, most of this may seem to be superfluous. However, a compass can be useful even then. If you go ashore in the evening, take a bearing on your boat, so that you can find your way back after dark. Nothing is more frustrating than rowing around an anchorage trying to find your boat among scores of others. Finally, a chart and compass, and knowing how to use them, is an essential safety element.

Chapter 9

MAINTENANCE

People are curious. They will spend tens of thousands of pounds on yachts and large motor boats, and further hundreds on maintaining them, but their tenders and dinghies are almost always neglected. Since even the smallest small boat is not cheap, it makes good sense from the financial as well as the safety point in view, to see that they are well maintained.

INFLATABLES

Every boat comes supplied with instructions telling the owner how to look after it. Read these instructions carefully. When inflating your boat, a hand, or foot pump is safer than an airline, and you should never exceed the recommended pressure, usually 2–2½ lbs. per square inch. Faulty assembly or inflation can damage your craft. It is more important not to over-inflate and, even if you use an airline to get air into the tubes, stop as soon as the boat has assumed its shape and complete the inflation with the manual or foot pump. If the inflatable boat is left in strong sunlight, you should mitigate the effects of heat expansion by releasing some of the air.

On coming ashore from the sea, sluice down the craft with fresh water and be sure to remove all sand or gravel from under the side tubes or bottom boards, where they will otherwise cause wear on the fabric.

All metal fittings should be lightly greased and every inflatable boat should be returned to the suppliers for servicing at least once a year.

DAMAGE

Inflatable boats are hard to damage, having built-in 'bounce'. A collision will usually occur on the bow, and a rope handling line, doubling as a lifeline is useful here.

Chafing and the odd puncture are possible and although most boats are furnished with one or more air compartments for safety, all punctures should be repaired as soon as possible.

A large rip must be sewn together before patching, and the patch must overlap the tear by at least 1½" all round. Clean off the area of the tear with fresh water and, after drying the area thoroughly, clean it with a solvent-like lighter fuel, but NOT a petrol mix, and then rub the surface down with a wire brush or

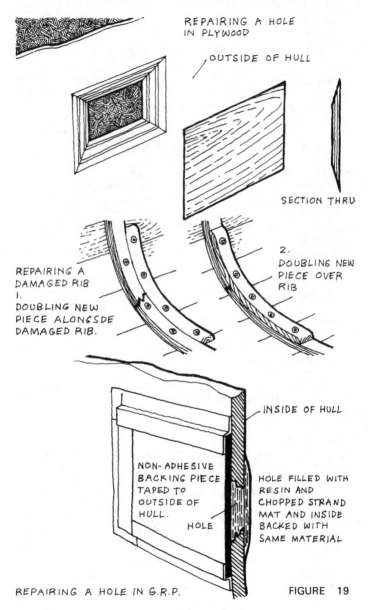

REPAIRING A HOLE
IN PLYWOOD

OUTSIDE OF HULL

SECTION THRU

REPAIRING A
DAMAGED RIB
1.
DOUBLING NEW
PIECE ALONGSDE
DAMAGED RIB.

2.
DOUBLING NEW
PIECE OVER
RIB

INSIDE OF HULL

NON-ADHESIVE
BACKING PIECE
TAPED TO
OUTSIDE OF
HULL.

HOLE

HOLE FILLED WITH
RESIN AND
CHOPPED STRAND
MAT AND INSIDE
BACKED WITH
SAME MATERIAL

REPAIRING A HOLE IN G.R.P.

FIGURE 19

glasspaper. Fix the patch in with tacky coatings of a neoprene adhesive and allow at least a day before you re-inflate the boat.

If you have a small leak, you can usually detect it by brushing the compartment with soapy water and looking for bubbles.

Make it a rule to check all the fittings on your boat regularly. Loose stitching, fraying ropes or a shaky outboard bracket will all subscribe to Murphy's Law, which states that anything that can go wrong, or break, will do so and at the most inconvenient moment.

WOODEN CRAFT

Maintenance is especially essential with wooden craft. The wet and especially sea water, will rapidly lead to mildew and rot. All craft should be allowed to dry out inboard, and compartments should be kept dry and aired. On the other hand, a wooden boat will stay watertight if kept afloat, and compartment hatches should not be left untended while the compartment 'airs', if this destroys the built-in buoyancy. Bare wood must be varnished or painted. Sand down wood and cover with primer, which is the main waterproofing agent, undercoat, paint or yacht enamel, rubbing down between coats. Always rub along the wood grain for varnish and diagonally for wood. Plywood must receive many coats, especially at the rough ends. These should be sanded down and varnished to prevent rot entering between the layers. As with inflatables, a sluicing down with fresh water after use will remove salt, mud and sand, which will otherwise remove the paint or varnish and expose the raw wood. Pay particular attention to rubbing strakes, oarlocks and fenders and the strakes along the bottom.

REPAIRS TO PLYWOOD

Small holes may be repaired by filling with glue and sawdust made into a paste and sanded down when set. Alternatively they may be filled using GRP.

A not too large hole can be repaired by trimming the hole to a neat rectangle and bevelling the edges so that the hole has a larger outside measurement than the inside one. Get a piece of marine ply and cut to the same shape. Clean off the paint or varnish from the surfaces to be fastened and then glue and screw the new piece into position. When dry, prime and finish as necessary.

REPAIRS TO HULLS

Repairs can be done by the owner if not too extensive. A cracked strake may be repaired by covering with a tingle, which is a piece of wood, curved at either end, either glued or screwed in place or fastened with copper nails. Sections of damaged planking can be replaced by cutting out the damaged plank and fixing a new section with glue and copper nails. A damaged rib may be repaired by fixing a new piece over the damaged area.

G.R.P.

Although G.R.P. does appear at first glance to be the perfect marine material, it can be damaged quite easily by banging, wear from ropes, dragging over shingle and by heat. Small holes can be repaired by using epoxy putty, with glue added for strength if necessary. Larger holed areas can be fixed by using Glass-matt, resin and hardener. First obtain a smooth surface to the outside and fill the area from within. If you use a brush, acetone will clean it, but you can use a rope end instead if you wish.

G.R.P. hardens with heat at 45°F (7°C). Below this temperature either increase the hardener or do repairs in a heated oven. Conversely, if you are doing the repair on a very hot day, you may find the work hardening too quickly. A dry day is best for using G.R.P., as it is for varnishing.

To prevent the hands from getting into too much of a mess use a barrier cream.

CORROSION

If two different metals are exposed to the air or immersed in sea water, a small electrical current is created and this in time will corrode them. The best cure is prevention, and this can be achieved by using compatable metals.

Corrosion can be slowed by fixing zinc anodes to the hull, but for small craft, it is as well to think of the possibilities of corrosion when fitting a bracket or screwing down a fitting, and check that the metals you employ are compatable. Your chandler or boat builder will give the necessary advice.

LAYING UP

Provided a craft is in frequent use and any small damage is treated as soon as it occurs, a good small boat will give years of service. Much more damage is done by neglect in the out-of-season period, or by failing to follow the necessary laying up procedures.

If the boat is left on a mooring, be sure that the mooring itself, the warps and anchors, are sufficient for rough weather. Dry out and air all compartments before closing and fit a 'tended' cover over the boat to shed the rain or spray. Remove all possible fittings, to a safe place, and carry out a full maintenance check within the shortest possible period, for example.

1. Inflatable craft to service agent.
2. Outboard engine to be cleaned, drained and serviced.
3. All fittings washed, repaired and placed in dry storage.
4. Check and repair all loose fittings.
5. Replace all safety equipment, flares etc.
6. Check insurance.

Chapter 10

SAFETY

Many small craft serve not only as tenders, but as life-rafts or safety vessels as well. Not all tenders are suitable for this purpose, and proper life-rafts, equipped with suitable gear, water and food, should be part of the equipment of any cruising yacht, or motor cruiser.

However, the vast majority of boating accidents take place between ship and shore, and if these could be eliminated or even reduced, then boating would be a much safer occupation.

The hazards are mainly due to ignorance or stupidity, but are usually directly due to one or more of the following causes:

1. Overloading.
2. Under-estimation of weather conditions (of sea, wind or tide).
3. Effect of alcohol.
4. Swamping by waves or wash.
5. Going too fast.
6. Engine failure — out of fuel and no alternative propulsion.
7. Running down.
8. Failure to display lights.
9. Failure to wear life-jackets.
10. Poor boat handling.

Some of these points we have already covered and some at considerable length. Prevention is always better than cure, but should things go wrong, it is as well to know what to do, so let us look at safety drills.

PRECAUTIONS

These may be listed as follows:
1. All aboard wear life-jackets.
2. Make more trips, rather than overload.
3. Don't go out having drunk too much. Stop anyone in liquor who intends to go out.
4. Study the sea and weather conditions.
5. Learn the rules for safe boat handling.
6. Have flares and lights aboard, especially at night.
7. Always have alternative propulsion.
8. Carry suitable equipment, bailers, anchors, line, safety lines on gunwhales.

9. Have a routine for coming alongside.
10. Be accomplished in small boat handling.

SWAMPING

If your boat is swamped and you have to take to the water STAY WITH THE BOAT and STAY TOGETHER.

Never let anyone, however strong a swimmer, strike out for the shore. When you are near another craft, shout for help TOGETHER.

An inflatable boat will not sink even if full of water, but loose equipment, oars, buckets, etc., can float away, so always have these tied in. Bail out enough to get someone aboard to bail out the craft and put the smallest, or oldest aboard first as their resistance to cold is less. Non-inflatable craft may still float and you can try gathering at the bow and rocking the boat until you have achieved enough buoyancy to put someone on board to bail. Continue to hold the boat head-on to the sea or current, so that it does not fill again. If the engine is swamped and stopped, use the oars or try sculling.

MAN OVERBOARD

If someone falls overboard, the one thing you *don't* do is Panic. Since the wind and weather offer such an endless variation of possibilities, we think it best just to stress a very few rules which everyone is agreed on.

FIGURE 20

HAUL INVOLUNTARY SWIMMER IN OVER THE STERN.
IT MAY BE NECESSARY TO PROVIDE A ROPE STIRRUP TO GET FOOT INTO.

First, don't panic. Second, keep your eye on the swimmer, or order someone else to do so while you go about. You can usually steer the boat quite well with your head over your shoulder. Third, run down on the swimmer as quickly as possible, and stop with the swimmer on the weather side. Doing this has several advantages. It stops the boat drifting down on the swimmer, and it may be more practical to get him aboard over the transom in spite of all the clutter there, and the wind or tide will help to hold him to the boat until you are ready to haul him aboard. Getting him *in* is the difficult bit, especially if he (let's assume it's a foolish man, ladies!) is cold and waterlogged. Get him to hold the side, take a deep breath, then push himself down neck deep in the water, and, while you lean out to lower the side, he heaves himself up. The buoyancy in his lungs and life jacket, plus a good heave and a pull from you, should have him sprawling on the bottom boards. Practise boarding or hauling someone over the side any time you go swimming off the boat.

SWIMMING AND DROWN-PROOFING

Everyone who enjoys the outdoors should be able to swim and tread water. Even a few strokes can save your life and today isn't too soon or late to start learning. However, in cold water, strong currents, or rough seas, even a strong swimmer may not last long.

In water of about 50°F (10°C) a man of average build would live about three hours. A fat man would last longer, and a small child much less. Swimming to stay warm is now considered to be worse than useless. Swimming exposes certain areas of the body, notably the groin, heart, lungs and neck to extreme heat loss and it is important that the swimmer conserves heat as much as possible by folding arms and legs closely to the body and staying as still as possible. Huddling close to a companion will also help. Some estimates state that these simple methods can increase survival time in the water by up to 50%, and so delay the onset of hypothermia. Life jackets, 'oilies' and all and any clothing also helps to maintain warmth, so stay clad, but alcohol is no help and should not be taken.

DISTRESS SIGNALS AND FLARES

In estuaries, or within the 3 mile limit, use red hand-flares or orange smoke to attract attention. Two-star red flares are useful at night, as are rockets. Do not fire off all your flares at once and preferably keep them until you are sure, or at least very hopeful of

FIGURE 21   DISTRESS SIGNALS

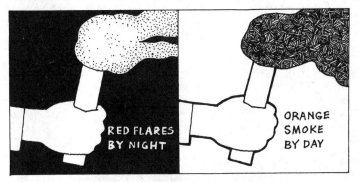

RED FLARES BY NIGHT

ORANGE SMOKE BY DAY

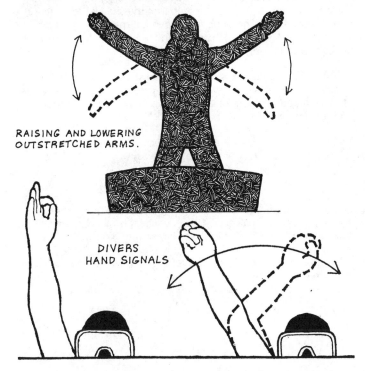

RAISING AND LOWERING OUTSTRETCHED ARMS.

DIVERS HAND SIGNALS

OK AT SURFACE

DISTRESS AT SURFACE

someone seeing them. Point the flares downwind, and if using rockets fire the first two within 2 minutes, so that any observers can check that a signal was actually seen. Use smoke flares when the rescuers are in sight.

HAND SIGNALS

Many small boats may not carry flares — although they should. In an emergency, waving an article of clothing on an oar is a distress signal, as is raising and lowering the outstretched arms. A black ball — a bundle of clothing or a fender hauled up the mast on the halyard is another distress signal.

HELICOPTERS

If a helicopter comes to your aid, help the crew and winchman. If applicable and possible, lower the mast. Steer into the wind and, if ordered to leave the craft and go into the sea by the helicopter winchman, do so. The winchman is in charge. Do not attach the winching wire or strap to the craft, and remember that the priority at this stage is to save *life*, not the boat.

FINALLY: A little knowledge is not always a dangerous thing, but more knowledge is never wasted. This book is part of a series, and to expand your knowledge may we refer you to other suitable and applicable titles, such as:

> *Weather Lore*
> *Knots, Bends & Hitches*
> *Chart and Compass*
> *Outdoor First Aid*

also in this series.

We hope that the information in this book will enable you to enjoy your boating much more fully and more safely in the future. courses arranged by the R.Y.A. your local or National Yachting Association, or a competent sailing school, will also be worth attending.

Whatever you do, take care of yourself, and good luck in all your ventures.